SPUD  MAN'S

SPUDTACULAR
BAKED
POTATO
COOKBOOK

SPUD MAN'S

SPUDTACULAR

BAKED POTATO COOKBOOK

Big portions, tasty toppings, can't lose

Harper
North

HarperNorth
Windmill Green
24 Mount Street
Manchester M2 3NX

HarperCollinsPublishers
1 London Bridge Street
London SE1 9GF

www.harpercollins.co.uk

HarperCollinsPublishers
Macken House
39/40 Mayor Street Upper
Dublin 1
D01 C9W8
Ireland

First published by
HarperCollinsPublishers 2024

1 3 5 7 9 10 8 6 4 2

Text © HarperCollins Publishers Ltd 2024
Photography © Georgie Glass 2024

Ben Newman aka Spud Man asserts the
moral right to be identified as the author
of this work

A catalogue record of this book is
available from the British Library

ISBN 978-0-00-872815-1

Photographer: Georgie Glass
Photography assistant: Sean McCrossan
Food Stylist: Lee-Ann Snyman
Assistant Food Stylist: Melanie Chlond
Props Stylist: Rebecca Hill
Art Direction: Rebecca Hill and Georgie Glass
Designer: Louise Leffler
Recipe developer: Heather Thomas

Printed in Latvia by PNB

MIX
Paper | Supporting
responsible forestry
FSC™ C007454

This book is produced from independently certified FSC™ paper
to ensure responsible forest management.

For more information visit: www.harpercollins.co.uk/green

For Sarah

In front of every good
Spud Man is a great Spud Wife

SPUD**CONTENTS**

SPUD **MAN: THE ORIGIN STORY** 9

SPUD**METHOD** 13

SPUD**SUPPLIERS** 15

SPUD**MATES** 15

SPUD**ESSENTIALS** 17

★ CHEESE AND BEANS 24

★ **CURRY, CHEESE AND CRISPY ONIONS** 27

★ THE COTTAGE PIE BAKED POTATO 28

★ **THE STEAK SPUD** 30

★ THE FISH PIE BAKED POTATO 35

★ **THE VEGAN CHILLI SPUD** 36

★ THE POUTINE-STYLE CHEESY SPUD 40

★ **THE MEATBALLS MARINARA SPUD** 42

★ THE MEGA MAC AND CHEESE SPUD 45

★ **THE LEBANESE CHICKEN SHAWARMA SPUD** 46

★ THE WORLD-FAMOUS CHEESE AND CHILLI 48

★ **THE BBQ PULLED PORK SPUD** 50

★ THE TERIYAKI CHICKEN ONE 54

★ **THE GREEK ONE** 56

★ THE FRENCH ONION ONE 61

★ **THE NEW YORKER** 62

★ THE WELSH ONE 65

★ **THE FOUR CHEESES** 68

What do you call a potato wearing glasses?

A spec-tater.

★ THE COLCANNON SPUD 73
★ THE HUMMUS ONE 74
★ THE THAI CURRY IN A HURRY 78
★ THE TUNA DELIGHT 80
★ THE CORONATION CHICKEN ONE 81
★ THE DEVILISH ONE 82
★ THE CURRYWURST SPUD 85
★ THE VEGGIE DELUXE 87
★ THE EGGS FLORENTINE 89
★ THE SMOKED SALMON AND CREAM CHEESE ONE 90
★ THE CHORIZO SHAKSHUKA 92
★ POSH BAKED BEANS 94
★ EASY CHEESY POTATO SKINS 99
★ PIZZA LOADED POTATO SKINS 103
★ LOADED BAKED POTATO NACHOS 104
★ TUNA MELT SPUDS 108
★ RED ONION AND GOAT'S CHEESE SKINS 111
★ SPICY GUAC AND SHRIMP SKINS 112
★ SAUSAGE AND MASH LOADED SKINS 114
★ CREAMY CHEESY TWICE-BAKED BRIE POTATOES 117
★ TEX-MEX LOADED SKINS 120
★ THE ONE, THE ONLY, ALL-DAY BREAKFAST SPUD 122

SPUDFACTS 124
SPUDJOKES 126
ACKNOWLEDGEMENTS 128

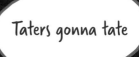

Taters gonna tate

SPUD MAN:
THE ORIGIN STORY

It was love at first sight for me and potatoes

But really, I was born into this. My dad was a potato merchant and he supplied pretty much 99 per cent of the potato vendors around the country, partly because he pre-wrapped his spuds in tin foil, which saved them a lot of time. No one does that any more. I used to go around with him and deliver them when I was a kid. So I grew up around potatoes. My grandad was a farmer as well. For as long as I can remember, I've been involved in the potato industry.

I've had the pitch on St Editha's Square in Tamworth since 2003, when I bought it from the previous owner, who was retiring. My dad had supplied him for over twenty years before I took it over, which is how I knew about it. I used to eat potatoes off this pitch as a kid.

At seventeen I was young, carefree and hungry so I thought, 'why not give it a go?'

I love this spot, next to the church and all the other traders here in beautiful Tamworth. This place was once capital of Mercia, one of three Anglo-Saxon kingdoms, and now it rules the spud kingdom.

Every day, every minute is nuts. On average, I prep 1,000 spuds on a weekday and 1,500 at a weekend. There are potatoes flying everywhere. It's gone intergalactic.

People have come from far and wide to try our spuds: from Australia, America and Canada. It's the greatest compliment. The other day a couple flew in from

PEOPLE HAVE COME FROM FAR AND WIDE TO TRY OUR SPUDS: FROM AUSTRALIA, AMERICA AND CANADA. IT'S THE GREATEST COMPLIMENT.

YOU SPUDFANS HAVE GIVEN ME SOME AMAZING OPPORTUNITIES. LIKE GOING TO SILVERSTONE FOR THE F1 AND MEETING RYAN REYNOLDS AND HUGH JACKMAN AT A FILM PREMIERE.

Malaysia, hired a car at Gatwick and drove straight to Tamworth to try my taters. How crazy is that?

Customer service is just as important to me as the product we sell. That's why we give some freebies away, and we always try to chat to people.

And loads of the people who turn up have never had a jacket potato before, so it's a big responsibility.

Everyone always thinks it's a winter food because it's warming, but we sell more in the summer when the weather's good and you can eat outside. And people tell me that the queue, the anticipation, is part of the experience. So thanks for waiting!

You SpudFans have given me some amazing opportunities. Like going to Silverstone for the F1 and meeting Ryan Reynolds and Hugh Jackman at a film premiere.

I've even been given an Honorary Freedom of the Borough, like some sort of medieval gentleman. It couldn't have happened anywhere but here in Tamworth.

I've been able to raise thousands for kidney charities too, which any regular viewers will know is a cause close to my heart. I've had three failed transplants and I can't have any more so I'll be on dialysis for the rest of my life. Hopefully I can show people that you can live a normal life, even with kidney failure.

I've got nine kids, so I expect we'll be able to keep the business in the family now, or for at least as long as people eat baked potatoes.

I probably consume at least three or four spuds a week myself, though if my doctor's reading this it's less than that because they're high in potassium and that's not good for me.

At home, I love a good roast dinner. You can't beat Spud Wife making a joint with all the trimmings on a Sunday.

SPUDMETHOD

Sometimes the simplest food is the hardest to get right, but I think I've perfected it.

The secret to baked potatoes is to cook them hot and fast. The crispier the better.

At home I do them unwrapped. The cooking time depends on the size of the potato, but if it fits in your hand, you should probably do them for about 1 hour 20 minutes at 220°C (fan 200°C).

Any larger, you're looking at more than 1 hour 30 minutes at least.

In the trailer we wrap them in tin foil and do them even hotter and even quicker. An industrial potato oven hits 300–350°C.

Don't always go for the largest potato you can find. A couple of smaller ones will cook more evenly and won't have any lumpy bits.

You don't need to prick them. That's a complete myth, and I've never seen a potato explode, like EV-ER.

Be patient and wait until they're ready. You can tell by giving the spud a little squeeze. If you feel like you could squeeze through it, it's ready. But it's got to have that give in it. We do it all by touch in the van, poking all of them. You need tough old hands.

What really makes baked potatoes the ultimate comfort food is butter. Lots of good quality butter, dripping out the side. Butter makes everything good, doesn't it?

Speed hack: microwave and then air fry your baked potato to ensure you still get a crispy skin.

Do not ever reheat a jacket potato. It's atrocious. Just eat it hot, and fast.

But really, it's not so much about how you cook the potato — it's the variety...

CHEESE
BBQ PULLED
PORK
SWEETCORN
TUNA MAYO
COLESLAW
BEANS
CHILLI
CON CARNE
CHICKEN CURRY
MINCED BEEF

DRINKS

TEA
COFFEE
CAPPUCCINO
HOT CHOCOLATE
COLD DRINKS

QUALITY
WASHED
POTATOES

Lowes Potato

LOWES POTATOES

15 KG

SPUDSUPPLIERS

THE SPUDS OF CHAMPIONS

All our potatoes come from the amazing guys at Lowe's Potatoes in Warwickshire (hello David, Jane, Nigel and Helen!), which is a third-generation family business founded in 1950. They supply all sorts of people including supermarkets, wholesalers, farm shops, local convenience stores, pubs and restaurants. There's every chance you've eaten one of their spuds without knowing. And they're bloody delicious.

We mainly use Marfona or Melody potatoes at the moment. Marfonas are versatile all-rounders, fresh with a nice yellow skin and flesh and a smooth, buttery texture packed full of flavour. I think they're from the Netherlands, originally. And Melodys have good taste and texture too, with smooth, clean skins. Cara is a good variety; we used to use Estimas too. Growing up with a potato merchant for a dad, I know my potatoes!

I'd generally advise against buying Nadine potatoes, which are often stocked by supermarkets. They look good and crop well but the cook is often poor.

BOOKER

Booker's is my happy place, and the source of so much of what I do and make. Thank you to everyone who has helped me over the years, and especially to Gill Shakeshaft and Kerry Drewett, Booker's development chef.

THE GRATE CHEESE COMPANY

Matt Grammer is my cheese man and has been for about twenty years. He's reliable, he rotates the stock and delivers early and on time. He's got me out of many a pickle, if you'll excuse the pun.

SPUDMATES

Shout out to **Wyldes Sweet Shop** on Lower Gungate and the OG Lydia Byron

Tip of the hat to **Birds Bakery**, discount sweets and snack store **Yum Yums**, **Tamworth News** and **Cosy Café**, not to mention **Tamworth Toolbox**.

Kudos to **Tamworth Borough Council** too, who really get it. They've been a great help, especially the one and only Michael Osborne.

And to all the people of Tamworth who have been my customers for the last twenty-odd years. Without you, I wouldn't be here.

SPUDESSENTIALS

Just some of the things every self-respecting spud maker should have in the cupboard

Balsamic vinegar
Beef stock cubes
Black pepper (freshly-ground)
Breadcrumbs (shop bought)
Brown sugar
Capers
Caster sugar
Cayenne pepper
Chilli flakes
Cider vinegar
Clear honey
Cornflour
Curry paste
Curry powder
Dried oregano
Flaked almonds
Garlic
Ground coriander
Ground cumin
Ground nutmeg
Harissa paste
Horseradish sauce
Mango chutney
Mayonnaise

Mustard (Dijon and wholegrain)
Olive oil
Paprika
Plain flour
Red wine vinegar
Roasted red peppers (jarred)
Root ginger
Salt
Soy sauce
Sriracha
Sundried tomato paste
Tabasco
Taco seasoning
Tahini
Thai sweet chilli sauce
Tinned Beans (cannellini,
butter beans or kidney beans)
Tinned sweetcorn
Tinned tuna (in spring water)
Tomato ketchup
Vegetable stock cubes
Walnuts
Worcestershire sauce

BUT BEFORE WE GET GOING, A BIT OF HOUSEKEEPING

1 When I say 'cheese', I usually mean our mix of cheese which is 80% Cheddar, 20% mozzarella. Unless I mention something else.

2 These recipes are intended for home cooking and small portions and therefore they'll be slightly different to the things you've seen me batch cook in the SpudWagon. In any case, some of those recipes are trade secrets so what you'll find here are recipes with a twist.

3 I'm told Americans don't call jacket spuds 'jacket spuds', so I only use the word 'baked' in this book. They're the same thing, though.

SPUDFACTS

More than 1 billion people worldwide eat potatoes and we produce > **375 million metric tons a year**

Spuds in Space:
In **1995**, the potato became the first vegetable ever grown in space!

World Champ Spud:
The heaviest potato ever recorded weighed a whopping **10 lb and 14 oz, or 4.98 kg!**

IT WAS LOVE AT FIRST SIGHT FOR ME AND POTATOES

THE
RECIPES

THE CHEESE AND BEANS: THE ORIGINAL AND STILL THE BEST

My Spud Man baked potatoes with heaps of baked beans and as much cheese as you can fit. They're easy to make and everyone loves them, especially the kids. Don't go easy on the butter.

Serves 2 | Prep: 10 minutes | Cook: 13–18 minutes

 2 x Spud Man baked potatoes

2 knobs of butter

115g (4oz) grated cheese

Homemade baked beans

1 tbsp olive oil

1 onion, diced

2 garlic cloves, crushed

1 x 400g (14oz) tin of chopped tomatoes

a good pinch of smoked paprika

a large pinch of dried oregano

a pinch of sugar

1 tbsp tomato paste

1 x 400g (14oz) tin of beans, e.g. cannellini, butter beans or kidney beans, rinsed and drained

a dash of cider vinegar

a handful of parsley, finely chopped

salt and freshly-ground black pepper

1 Make the baked beans: heat the olive oil in a saucepan set over a low to medium heat. Add the onion and garlic and cook for 6 minutes, stirring occasionally, until tender.

2 Stir in the tomatoes, smoked paprika, oregano and sugar and cook for 5–10 minutes over a medium heat until the mixture thickens and reduces. Add the tomato paste and beans and warm through gently. Add a few drops of cider vinegar to taste, the chopped parsley and some salt and pepper.

3 Cut a large cross in the top of each spud and press gently on the sides to open it up. Mash in the butter and spoon the baked beans over the top. Sprinkle with lots of grated cheese and enjoy.

 If you're in a hurry and don't want to faff around making your own baked beans, just open a tin and warm the beans through.

THE CURRY, CHEESE AND CRISPY ONIONS ONE

One of my best-loved baked spuds — a classic in the Spud Man repertoire. The chicken curry is easy-peasy to make. It freezes well, so you could make double or treble the quantity and spoon into freezer bags for topping future jackets. You can buy packs of crispy onions in most supermarkets.

Serves 2 | Prep: 10 minutes | Cook: 40—50 minutes

 **2 x Spud Man baked potatoes**

2 large knobs of butter

60g (2oz) grated cheese

loads of crispy onions

salt and freshly-ground black pepper

Chicken curry

2 tbsp vegetable oil

1 large onion, thinly sliced

3 garlic cloves, crushed

2.5cm (1in) piece of fresh ginger, peeled and grated

4 skinned boneless chicken thighs, cut into cubes

2 tbsp curry paste

1 tsp ground coriander

1 tsp ground cumin

1 tsp ground turmeric

½ tsp ground cinnamon

200ml (7fl oz) chicken stock

1 x 400g (14oz) tin of chopped tomatoes

200ml (7fl oz) tinned coconut milk

1 Make the chicken curry: heat the oil in a large saucepan set over a medium heat. Add the onion and cook, stirring occasionally, for 8 minutes, or until tender and golden brown. Stir in the garlic and ginger and cook for 2 minutes.

2 Stir in the chicken and cook for 5 minutes, or until it's just starting to colour. Stir in the curry paste and ground spices and cook for 1—2 minutes.

3 Add the chicken stock and tomatoes, and bring to the boil. Reduce the heat to low and add the coconut milk. Cook gently for 20—30 minutes, or until the chicken is cooked and tender, and the curry has reduced and thickened. Add salt and pepper if needed.

4 Cut a big cross in the top of each spud and press gently on the sides to open it up. Add a big knob of butter and mash it in with a fork, then season with plenty of salt and pepper.

5 Spoon the curry over the baked potatoes and sprinkle with loads of grated cheese and crispy onions. Enjoy!!

THE COTTAGE PIE
BAKED POTATO

This is a sensational two-in-one recipe and these spuds taste as good as they look. You can make the minced beef filling in advance and keep it in a sealed container in the fridge until you're ready to go.

Serves 2 | Prep: 20 minutes | Cook: 40 minutes

 2 x Spud Man baked potatoes

Cottage pie filling

1 tbsp olive oil

1 onion, finely chopped

2 sticks celery, chopped

1 large carrot, chopped

200g (7oz) minced beef

200ml (7fl oz) hot beef stock

a handful of frozen peas

2 tbsp tomato ketchup (or tomato paste)

1 tbsp Worcestershire sauce

2 tsp cornflour

15g (½oz) butter

½ tsp wholegrain or Dijon mustard

60g (2oz) grated cheese

salt and freshly-ground black pepper

1 Make the cottage pie filling: heat the oil in a saucepan set over a medium heat. Cook the onion, celery and carrot, stirring occasionally, for 5 minutes, or until softened. Stir in the mince and cook for 5 minutes until browned all over.

2 Stir in the stock, frozen peas, ketchup (or tomato paste) and Worcestershire sauce, then season with salt and pepper. Reduce the heat and simmer for 10 minutes, or until the sauce reduces. In a small bowl, mix the cornflour with a little water to a smooth paste. Stir into the minced beef mixture and cook gently for 1–2 minutes until thickened.

3 Meanwhile, preheat the oven to 200°C (fan 180°C).

4 Cut the cooked spuds in half and scoop out the flesh, leaving a 5mm (¼ in) thick shell. Transfer the flesh to a bowl and mash with the butter. Beat in the mustard and grated cheese, then season to taste with salt and pepper.

5 Divide the minced beef mixture between the potato shells and cover with the mashed potato, roughing it up with a fork. Place on a baking tray.

6 Bake in the preheated oven for 15 minutes until the potato is crispy and golden brown.

These gorgeous spuds are even better served with loads of gravy and some green veg, such as sprouts, cabbage or broccoli.

THE STEAK SPUD

This beats steak and chips hands down! And it's much less fiddly and a bit healthier too. You can cook the steaks to your own preference, from rare to well done. Anything goes.

Serves 2 | Prep: 10 minutes | Cook: 20 minutes

 **2 x Spud Man baked potatoes**

2 x 150g (5½oz) lean rump or sirloin steaks

olive oil, for brushing

2 large knobs of butter

mustard, horseradish, Worcestershire sauce or béarnaise sauce

salt and freshly-ground black pepper

Fried onions and mushrooms

2 tbsp olive oil

a knob of butter

2 large onions, sliced into thin rounds

200g (7oz) button or chestnut mushrooms, sliced

1 Make the fried onions and mushrooms: heat the oil and butter in a frying pan set over a medium heat and add the onions. Cook, stirring occasionally, for 15 minutes, or until they are soft and golden brown. Remove from the pan and keep warm.

2 Add the mushrooms to the pan and cook, turning occasionally, for 5 minutes or until tender and golden brown. Remove and keep warm.

3 Meanwhile, lightly brush the steaks with oil and season with plenty of salt and pepper. Set a heavy frying pan or ridged griddle pan over a high heat and when it's smoking hot add the steaks. Sear for 2–3 minutes each side for rare to medium-rare – longer if you like them well done. Remove from the pan and leave to rest on a chopping board.

4 Cut a big cross in the top of each spud and press gently on the sides to open it up. Add a big knob of butter and season with plenty of salt and pepper. Pile the fried onions and mushrooms on top.

5 Cut the warm steaks into thin slices and arrange on top of the onions and mushrooms. Serve immediately with lashings of mustard, horseradish, Worcestershire sauce or béarnaise sauce, or treat yourself to a combo of all four!

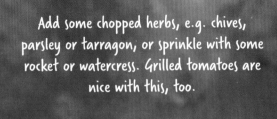

Add some chopped herbs, e.g. chives, parsley or tarragon, or sprinkle with some rocket or watercress. Grilled tomatoes are nice with this, too.

THE FISH PIE BAKED POTATO

Nothing beats a tasty fish pie supper when you're craving comfort food, especially on a cold day, so why not try my quick and easy take on a classic? Use baked spuds instead of mash and stuff them with a supermarket pie mix and some lovely grated Cheddar. Immense.

Serves 2 | Prep: 15 minutes | Cook: 15–20 minutes

 **2 x Spud Man baked potatoes**

Fish pie filling

200ml (7fl oz) milk or fish stock

225g (8oz) fish pie mix, e.g. salmon, smoked haddock and cod fillets, cut into small chunks

3–4 tbsp sour cream or Greek yoghurt

a small handful of parsley or chives, chopped

30g (1oz) butter

½ tsp wholegrain or Dijon mustard

60g (2oz) grated cheese

salt and freshly-ground black pepper

Add some peeled prawns or cooked peas for extra colour and flavour. Yum!

1 Preheat the oven to 200°C (fan 180°C).

2 Make the fish pie filling: warm the milk or fish stock in a pan set over a low heat. Add the fish and simmer gently for 4–5 minutes until tender and just cooked.

3 Remove the fish with a slotted spoon and transfer to a bowl. Add the sour cream or yoghurt and the chopped herbs, then stir gently to avoid flaking the fish.

4 Cut the cooked spuds in half and scoop out the flesh, leaving a 5mm (¼inch) thick shell. Put the flesh into a bowl and mash it with the butter. Beat in the mustard and grated cheese, then season with salt and pepper.

5 Divide the fish mixture between the potato shells and cover with the mashed potato, roughing it up with a fork. Place on a baking tray.

6 Bake in the preheated oven for 15–20 minutes until appetizingly crisp and golden brown on top.

THE VEGAN CHILLI SPUD

I'm basically a meat and potatoes man, but I enjoy my veggies and sometimes I like to eat this easy-peasy vegan chilli with tinned beans. It takes very little time to make and keeps well in a covered container in the fridge for up to three days.

Serves 2 | Prep: 15 minutes | Cook: 20—25 minutes

 **2 x Spud Man baked potatoes**

2 big dollops of guacamole or some diced avocado

coconut or soya yoghurt (optional)

Vegan chilli

2 tbsp olive oil

1 large red onion, thinly sliced

1 red pepper, seeds removed, chopped small

2 garlic cloves, crushed

1 tsp ground cumin

1 tsp smoked paprika

1 tsp chilli powder

1 red or green chilli, chopped small

1 x 400g (14oz) tin of chopped tomatoes

½ tsp sugar

1 x 400g (14oz) tin of black beans, rinsed and drained

juice of 1 lime

a handful of coriander, chopped

salt and freshly-ground black pepper

1 Heat the olive oil in a saucepan set over a low to medium heat and cook the onion, red pepper and garlic, stirring occasionally, for 8 minutes, or until softened. Stir in the ground spices, chilli powder and chopped chilli and cook for 1 minute.

2 Add the tomatoes, sugar and beans and cook gently for 10—15 minutes, or until thickened and reduced. Season to taste with salt and pepper and stir in the lime juice and most of the coriander.

3 Cut a big cross in the top of each spud and press gently on the sides to open it up. Season with plenty of salt and pepper and pour the vegan chilli over the top.

4 Add some guacamole or avocado and sprinkle with the remaining coriander. Serve, if wished, with some soya or coconut yoghurt.

You can substitute red kidney beans for the black beans, or any other tinned beans — even chickpeas that are lurking in your kitchen cupboard. If you don't like coriander, use parsley instead.

THE POUTINE-STYLE CHEESY SPUD

If you've never eaten spuds with melted cheese and gravy, you don't know what you've been missing. They're dead easy to make and everyone loves them. You don't even have to make fresh gravy if you're in a hurry — reheat some leftover gravy from the Sunday roast or buy some.

Serves 2 | Prep: 10 minutes | Cook: 25 minutes

 **2 x Spud Man baked potatoes**

Poutine topping

2 tbsp butter

2–3 tbsp milk

2 tbsp sour cream

1 tsp Dijon mustard

60g (2oz) grated cheese (try Gruyère if you want to try something different)

60g (2oz) shredded mozzarella

chopped chives and cayenne pepper

Gravy

2 tbsp olive oil

1 onion, thinly sliced

1 tbsp plain flour

150ml (5fl oz) beef, chicken or vegetable stock

1–2 tbsp balsamic vinegar

a dash of Worcestershire sauce

salt and freshly-ground black pepper

To make this even tastier, top with some caramelized fried onions and crumbled crispy bacon rashers.

1 Preheat the oven to 200°C (fan 180°C).

2 Make the gravy: heat the olive oil in a frying pan set over a low heat. Cook the onion for 15 minutes, stirring occasionally, until tender and starting to caramelize. Stir in the flour and cook for 1 minute. Add the stock, vinegar and Worcestershire sauce, then bring to the boil, stirring. Reduce the heat and let the gravy bubble gently for 4–5 minutes until thickened and smooth. Season to taste.

3 Meanwhile make the poutine topping. Cut the cooked spuds in half and scoop out the flesh, leaving a 5mm ((¼in) thick shell. Transfer the flesh to a bowl and mash with the butter, milk and sour cream. Season with salt and pepper, then beat in the mustard and grated cheese.

4 Divide the mixture between the potato shells and place them in an ovenproof baking dish.

5 Bake in the preheated oven for 15 minutes, or until crispy and golden brown. Pour some of the gravy over the top and sprinkle with the mozzarella. Return to the oven for 5 minutes, or until the cheese melts.

6 Serve immediately, sprinkled with chives and dusted with cayenne, with the remaining gravy on the side.

THE MEATBALLS MARINARA SPUD

Is there anyone who doesn't like meatballs and tomato sauce? Of course not . . . unless you're vegetarian. I enjoy large portions but you may find that there's too much sauce and meatballs for two people. Any leftovers, freeze them for another day or enjoy them with spaghetti.

Serves 2 | Prep: 15 minutes | Cook: 25–30 minutes

 2 x Spud Man baked potatoes

olive oil

2 knobs of butter

grated Parmesan cheese

Meatballs

450g (1lb) minced beef

30g (1oz) fresh white breadcrumbs

50g (1¾oz) grated Parmesan cheese

2 garlic cloves, crushed

a handful of parsley, finely chopped

3 tbsp olive oil

1 small onion, grated

1 egg, beaten

salt and freshly-ground black pepper

Marinara sauce

4 tbsp olive oil

5 garlic cloves, crushed

2 x 400g (14oz) tins of plum tomatoes

a pinch of crushed chilli flakes

a pinch of dried oregano

1 Make the meatballs: mix all the ingredients together in a bowl, adding enough beaten egg to bind the mixture together. Season with salt and pepper.

2 Take a small amount of the mixture in your hands and roll it into a ball. Repeat with the remaining mixture. Cover the meatballs and chill in the fridge while you make the marinara sauce.

3 Make the marinara sauce: heat the oil in a large frying pan set over a medium heat. Cook the garlic, stirring, for 1–2 minutes, without colouring, and then add the tomatoes together with a tinful of water. Crush the tomatoes gently with a wooden spoon and then stir in the chilli flakes, oregano and some salt and pepper.

4 Cook gently for 15–20 minutes, or until the sauce thickens and reduces. If it's bubbling too fast, reduce the heat as low as it will go – you just want a gentle simmer.

What do you call a lazy spud?
A couch potato!

5 While the sauce is simmering away, fry the meatballs: heat the olive oil in a frying pan set over a medium heat and cook the meatballs for 4–5 minutes until well browned underneath. Turn them over and brown the other side. Remove with a slotted spoon and drain on kitchen paper.

6 Cut a big cross in the top of each spud and press gently on the sides to open it up. Mash in the butter with a fork and season with salt and pepper. Place each potato in a shallow serving bowl.

7 Divide the meatballs between the potatoes and pour the marinara sauce over the top. Sprinkle with loads of cheese and dig in.

Make double the quantity of meatballs and sauce and freeze them for a future date when you don't have much time to cook.

THE MEGA MAC AND CHEESE SPUD

My mac and cheese baked spuds are the ultimate comfort food. They're so easy to make and you can cook the macaroni and the white sauce while the spuds are baking. A proper feast!

Serves 2 | Prep: 5 minutes | Cook: 25–30 minutes

2 x Spud Man baked potatoes

200g (7oz) dried macaroni

2 knobs of butter

50g (1¾oz) grated cheese

olive oil

White sauce

50g (1¾oz) butter

30g (1oz) plain flour

350ml (12fl oz) milk

50g (1¾oz) grated Cheddar cheese

1 tsp Dijon mustard

salt and freshly-ground black pepper

For an even crunchier topping, sprinkle some breadcrumbs over the top before popping the spuds into the oven.

1 Preheat the oven to 190°C (fan 170°C).

2 Cook the macaroni in a large pan of lightly salted boiling water according to the packet instructions. Drain and keep warm.

3 Meanwhile, make the white sauce: melt the butter in a non-stick pan set over a low heat and stir in the flour. Cook for 2 minutes until it forms a smooth paste and then add the milk, a little at a time, stirring or whisking until smooth. Keep stirring over a low heat until the sauce thickens. Stir in the cheese and mustard and cook for 1 minute. Season with salt and pepper, then stir in the cooked macaroni.

4 Cut a big cross in the top of each spud and press gently on the sides to open it up. Add a big knob of butter and mash it in with a fork, then season with plenty of salt and pepper. Place in an ovenproof dish and spoon the macaroni cheese mixture over the top. Sprinkle with the grated cheese and drizzle with some olive oil.

5 Bake in the preheated oven for 15–20 minutes, until bubbling, crisp and golden brown.

THE LEBANESE CHICKEN SHAWARMA SPUD

This is for all the garlic fans out there. A kebab on a spud: that's the stuff dreams are made of. Dead easy to make and absolutely mint.

Serves 2 | Prep: 10 minutes | Chill: 15 minutes | Cook: 10—13 minutes

 **2 x Spud Man baked potatoes**

Chicken shawarma topping

3–4 garlic cloves, crushed

½ tsp ground cumin

½ tsp ground coriander

2 tbsp olive oil

juice of ½ lemon

250g (9oz) chicken breasts, cut into strips

1 small red pepper, seeds removed, thinly sliced

1 red onion, thinly sliced

4 tbsp fat-free Greek yoghurt

a few sprigs of parsley, chopped

a good pinch of paprika

salt and freshly-ground black pepper

1 In a bowl, mix together the garlic, ground spices, 1 tablespoon olive oil and the lemon juice. Season with salt and pepper and add the chicken, turning it in the marinade. Cover and chill in the fridge for at least 15 minutes.

2 Heat the remaining oil in a griddle pan set over a medium to high heat and cook the red pepper and onion, turning occasionally, for 4–5 minutes, until tender and slightly charred. Remove from the pan and set aside.

3 Add the chicken to the pan and cook, turning occasionally, for 6–8 minutes, until cooked through and golden brown.

4 Meanwhile, cut a large cross in the top of each spud and gently squeeze the bottom to open the top. Place each one in a bowl.

5 Gently mix the chicken and griddled vegetables with the yoghurt and spoon into and over the top of the potatoes. Sprinkle with parsley, dust with paprika and enjoy!

These spuds taste great served with a Lebanese salad: make with diced tomatoes, green pepper, cucumber, spring onions and parsley tossed in an olive oil and lemon dressing.

THE WORLD-FAMOUS CHEESE AND CHILLI

This is as good as it gets – it's spicy, it's comforting, it's filling. The chilli is enough to top two large potatoes, but you could make double the quantity and heat up any leftovers with some rice the following day.

Serves 2 | Prep: 10 minutes | Cook: 40 minutes

2 x Spud Man baked potatoes

2 knobs of butter

114g (4oz) grated cheese, e.g. Cheddar or Monterey Jack

a few sprigs of coriander or parsley, chopped

a big dollop of sour cream or Greek yoghurt

Spud Man's chilli

1 tbsp olive oil

1 onion, finely chopped

225g (8oz) lean minced beef

1 tsp garlic powder or flakes

1 tsp crushed chilli flakes

1 tsp ground cumin

1 tsp sweet paprika

½ tsp ground cinnamon

½ tsp dried oregano

½ tsp dried thyme

400g (14oz) tin of chopped tomatoes

240ml (8fl oz) hot beef stock

400g (14oz) tin of pinto or kidney beans, rinsed and drained

100g (3½oz) tinned sweetcorn, drained

150g (5oz) tinned baked beans

salt and freshly-ground black pepper

1 Make Spud Man's chilli: heat the oil in a saucepan set over a low to medium heat. Sweat the onion, stirring occasionally, for 10 minutes, or until really tender.

2 Stir in the minced beef, garlic, chilli, ground spices and herbs and cook, stirring occasionally, for 5 minutes, or until the bèef is browned all over. Add the tomatoes and stock and bring to the boil.

3 Reduce the heat to low and add the pinto beans and sweetcorn. Simmer gently for 25 minutes or until the beef is cooked, the vegetables are tender and the sauce has reduced and thickened. Season with salt and pepper.

4 Cut a big cross in the top of each spud and press gently on the sides to open it up. Mash in a knob of butter with a fork and season with plenty of salt and pepper.

5 Spoon the chilli over the top and sprinkle with the grated cheese and chopped coriander or parsley. Add a large dollop of sour cream or yoghurt and devour – don't hang about!

 Add some guacamole or diced avocado or even some crushed tortilla chips as a garnish. Or sprinkle with some sliced jalapeños. Whatever rocks your boat . . .

THE BBQ PULLED PORK SPUD

My pulled pork spuds with lashings of homemade BBQ sauce are monsters! It's well worth preparing and cooking the pulled pork in advance. Of course, you can cheat and use readymade BBQ sauce from the supermarket. I serve mine with a homemade coleslaw but anything goes — top with crispy onions or bacon bits, or add a big dollop of guacamole.

Serves 2 | Prep: 15 minutes | Chill: 4–5 hours | Cook: 2¾–3¼ hours

 2 x Spud Man baked potatoes

2 knobs of butter

85g (3oz) grated cheese (you could use Monterey Jack)

sliced spring onions and jalapeños

coleslaw (see page 62)

Pulled pork topping

2 tsp light brown sugar

2 tsp sweet paprika

1 tsp ground cumin

1–2 tsp chilli powder

½ tsp cayenne pepper

500g (1lb 2oz) boneless pork shoulder

1–2 tbsp vegetable oil

salt and freshly-ground black pepper

Smoky BBQ sauce

300ml (½ pint) tomato ketchup

3 tbsp light brown sugar

3 tbsp red wine or cider vinegar

2 tbsp Worcestershire sauce

1 tbsp soy sauce

1 tbsp Dijon or wholegrain mustard

juice of ½ lemon

1–2 tsp smoked paprika

½ tsp garlic powder

You can make the pulled pork and BBQ sauce in advance and store them in sealed containers in the fridge for up to 24 hours before reheating and topping the spuds.

1 Make the pulled pork topping: in a bowl, mix together the sugar and ground spices with some salt and pepper to make a dry rub. Spread it over the pork, then wrap it in kitchen foil and chill in the fridge for 4–5 hours.

2 Remove the pork from the fridge and bring it up to room temperature. Preheat the oven to 160°C (fan 140°C).

3 Heat the oil in a large casserole dish over a medium heat and sear the pork until browned all over. Cover with a lid and cook in the preheated oven for 2½–3 hours, or until the meat is really tender and falling apart.

4 While the meat is cooking, make the smoky BBQ sauce: put all the ingredients in a small saucepan and stir well. Put over a medium heat and when the sauce starts to bubble gently, give it a stir and cook for 5 minutes. Add salt and pepper to taste. Shred the cooked pork into the BBQ sauce with a fork and stir until coated all over.

5 Cut the cooked spuds in half and scoop out the flesh, leaving a 5mm ((¼in) thick shell. Transfer to a bowl and mash it with the butter. Season with salt and pepper and beat in most of the grated cheese.

6 Spoon the cheesy mash into the potato shells and place in two heatproof bowls. Top with the BBQ pulled pork and sprinkle the remaining grated cheese over the top. Pop under a preheated overhead grill on high for 5–10 minutes, or until the cheese melts.

7 Serve immediately, sprinkled with spring onions and jalapeños and topped with a large spoonful of coleslaw.

THE SECRET TO
BAKED POTATOES
IS TO DO THEM
HOT AND FAST.
THE CRISPIER
THE BETTER.

THE TERIYAKI CHICKEN ONE

Feel like something spicy and meaty? Try my spuds topped with sticky teriyaki chicken. Making your own sauce is worth the effort. It only takes five minutes and tastes loads better than the stuff in a jar.

Serves 2 | Prep: 10 minutes | Chill: 1 hour | Cook: 20 minutes

 *2 x Spud Man baked potatoes*

350g (12oz) skinned, boneless chicken thighs, cut into cubes

2 tsp olive or sesame oil

sesame seeds, for sprinkling

2 knobs of butter

chopped red chillies and spring onions

hot chilli sauce (optional)

salt and freshly-ground black pepper

Teriyaki sauce

4 tbsp soy sauce

2 tbsp mirin

1 tbsp clear honey

1 tbsp light brown sugar

2 tsp grated fresh ginger

2 garlic cloves, crushed

1 Make the teriyaki sauce: mix all the ingredients together in a large bowl. Add the chicken and stir well until the cubes are coated all over with the marinade. Cover and chill in the fridge for at least 1 hour.

2 To cook the chicken, heat the oil in a frying pan set over a medium heat. When it's hot, lift the chicken out of the marinade and cook, turning occasionally, for 15 minutes. Add the remaining marinade to the pan and cook for 4–5 minutes until the sauce reduces and the chicken is glossy. Remove from the pan and sprinkle with sesame seeds.

3 Cut a big cross in the top of each spud and press gently on the sides to open it up. Add a knob of butter and season with plenty of salt and pepper.

4 Spoon the teriyaki chicken over the top, then sprinkle with chillies and spring onions. Serve immediately, drizzled with chilli sauce (optional).

 You can cook the chicken in an air fryer. Just place in a single layer in the air fryer and cook for 12–15 minutes, turning it over after 6 minutes. It's ready when it's cooked right through.

THE GREEK ONE

These are some absolutely banging spuds. They're fresh, zingy and taste like holidays. The homemade tzatziki is awesome but if you don't have time to make it yourself, just use a tub of readymade from the supermarket.

Serves 2 | Prep: 15 minutes

 **2 x Spud Man baked potatoes**

Greek salad topping

2 juicy ripe tomatoes, seeds removed, chopped small

¼ red onion, thinly sliced

½ green pepper, seeds removed, chopped

8 black olives, stones removed and chopped

1 tsp extra virgin olive oil

1 tsp red wine vinegar

a good pinch of dried oregano

60g (2oz) feta cheese

salt and freshly-ground black pepper

Tzatziki

200g (7oz) Greek yoghurt

1 tsp olive oil

½ small cucumber, chopped small

2 garlic cloves, crushed

a few sprigs of mint and dill, chopped

grated zest and juice of ½ lemon

1 Make the tzatziki: mix all the ingredients together in a bowl and season with salt and pepper. Cover and pop in the fridge while you make the topping.

2 Make the Greek salad topping: put the tomatoes, onion, green pepper and olives in a bowl. Add the oil and vinegar and mix well. Stir in the oregano and season with salt and pepper.

3 Cut a large cross in the top of each spud and gently squeeze the bottom to open the top. Spoon the Greek salad topping into and over the potatoes and crumble the feta over the top.

4 Serve immediately with a large dollop of tzatziki on the side.

Add some capers or chopped cucumber to the Greek salad mixture.

THE FRENCH ONION ONE

On a cold day, nothing beats my sweet and sticky caramelized onion baked spuds, with a bubbling cheesy topping. Try them and see for yourself how good they are. They're sure to become a firm family favourite.

Serves 2 | Prep: 10 minutes | Cook: 45–60 minutes

 2 x Spud Man baked potatoes

2 large knobs of butter

a few sprigs of parsley, chopped

115g (4oz) Gruyère cheese, grated

1 tsp Dijon mustard

salt and freshly-ground black pepper

Caramelized fried onions

15g (½oz) unsalted butter

2 tbsp olive oil

2 large red onions, thinly sliced

3 garlic cloves, crushed

1 tbsp red wine vinegar

2 tbsp light brown sugar

1 Make the caramelized fried onions: heat the butter and olive oil in a large frying pan set over a low heat. Add the onions and cook very slowly and gently for 30–40 minutes, stirring occasionally, until they are tender and golden brown and starting to caramelize. Watch them carefully in case they start to burn.

2 Stir in the garlic and cook for 1 minute, and then add the vinegar and sugar. Cook gently for 5 minutes, stirring until the sugar dissolves.

3 Preheat the oven to 200°C (fan 180°C).

4 Cut a big cross in the top of each spud and press gently on the sides to open it up. Scoop out some of the cooked potato inside and mash it with the butter. Mix in some of the fried onions, the parsley, half of the grated cheese and the mustard. Season with salt and pepper to taste.

5 Divide the mixture between the potato skins and place in an ovenproof dish. Top with the rest of the fried onions and sprinkle with the remaining cheese.

6 Bake in the preheated oven for 10–15 minutes until the cheese has melted and is golden brown and bubbling.

I've used red onions because they have a higher sugar content than white ones and caramelize well. But white and brown onions work too.

THE NEW YORKER

Based on the classic Reuben sandwich beloved of New Yorkers, this is filling and warming on a cold day when you're craving something hot and delicious. Tight!

Serves 2 | Prep: 15 minutes | Cook: 8–10 minutes

 **2 x Spud Man baked potatoes**

2 large knobs of butter

115g (4oz) pastrami, diced

2 dill pickles, thinly sliced or diced

85g (3oz) grated Swiss cheese, e.g. Emmenthal or Gruyère

a few sprigs of parsley, chopped

mustard or tomato ketchup (optional)

Coleslaw

200g (7oz) mixed red and white cabbage, thinly sliced

2 carrots, grated

a bunch of spring onions, thinly sliced

1 red apple, cored and chopped small

30g (1oz) walnuts, chopped

a handful of parsley, chopped

115g (4oz) mayonnaise

juice of ½ lemon

salt and freshly-ground black pepper

1 Make the coleslaw: put the cabbage, carrots, spring onions, apple, walnuts and parsley in a bowl and mix together. Gently stir in the mayonnaise and lemon juice and season with salt and pepper. Cover and chill in the fridge until needed.

2 Preheat the oven to 190°C (fan 170°C).

3 Cut a big cross in the top of each spud and press gently on the sides to open it up as wide as possible. Add a big knob of butter and season with plenty of salt and pepper, then fluff up with a fork.

4 Place the potatoes on a baking tray and top with the pastrami and dill pickles. Cover with the grated cheese and bake in the preheated oven for 8–10 minutes until the cheese has melted and is golden brown and bubbling.

5 Sprinkle the potatoes with the parsley and serve with some coleslaw piled on top and mustard or tomato ketchup on the side (optional).

A traditional Reuben sandwich is made with corned beef and sauerkraut, so try substituting these for the pastrami and coleslaw.

THE WELSH ONE

This is my take on a baked spud and Welsh rarebit combo. Some hard Caerphilly cheeses grate well, but you can crumble them into the sauce and over the top if you prefer. It's a good melting cheese with a mild flavour, so you may want to add plenty of mustard and Worcestershire sauce to spice it up!

Serves 2 | Prep: 10 minutes | Cook: 25–35 minutes

 2 x Spud Man baked potatoes

2 knobs of butter

30g (1oz) Caerphilly cheese, grated

Cheesy leek filling

50g (1¾oz) butter

2 leeks, washed, trimmed and sliced

2 garlic cloves, crushed (optional)

2–3 heaped tbsp plain flour

300ml (½ pint) milk

100g (3½oz) Caerphilly cheese, grated

1 tsp mustard

a dash of Worcestershire sauce

salt and freshly-ground black pepper

1 Preheat the oven to 190°C (fan 170°C).

2 Make the cheesy leek filling: heat the butter in a saucepan set over a low to medium heat. Add the leeks and cook, stirring frequently, for 8–10 minutes, until they are tender and golden. If using, stir in the garlic and cook for 1–2 minutes.

3 Stir in the flour and cook, stirring occasionally, until you have a smooth paste. Add the milk gradually, stirring all the time, and then turn up the heat. When the sauce starts to boil, reduce the heat to low and cook gently for 3–4 minutes until thickened and smooth. Stir in the grated cheese and mustard and cook for 1 minute. Season to taste with Worcestershire sauce, salt and pepper.

4 Cut a big cross in the top of each spud and press gently on the sides to open it up. Scoop out some of the cooked potato inside and mash it into the cheesy leek sauce.

5 Mash a knob of butter into each baked potato skin with a fork, then season with salt and pepper. Pile the cheesy leek and potato mixture back into each potato skin, and sprinkle with grated Caerphilly. Place in an ovenproof dish.

6 Bake in the preheated oven for 10–15 minutes until crisp and golden brown.

If you don't have Caerphilly, use Cheddar or Swiss cheese. You can also sprinkle with some crispy bacon bits.

WHY DOES EVERYONE LOVE COOKING WITH POTATOES?

BECAUSE THEY'RE VERY A-PEELING.

THE FOUR CHEESES

One of the absolute best but only for the very brave. These spuds are oozing with stringy, gooey melted cheese for that signature cheese pull. Use only cheeses that melt well (see below), so forget about halloumi, feta and other fancy cheeses. And if you use Cheddar, opt for a mild one, which melts better than the punchier medium and mature varieties.

Serves 2 | Prep: 10 minutes | Cook: 20 minutes

 **2 x Spud Man baked potatoes**

60g (2oz) butter

1–2 tsp French mustard

400g (14oz) grated cheese, e.g. mild Cheddar, Gruyère, mozzarella and Monterey Jack or chopped Brie or Camembert (rind removed)

chopped spring onions and chives

sour cream or Greek yoghurt (optional)

salt and freshly-ground black pepper

1 Preheat the oven to 200°C (fan 180°C).

2 Cut the cooked spuds in half and scoop out the flesh, leaving a 5mm (¼in) thick shell. Transfer the flesh to a bowl and mash it with the butter. Beat in the mustard and half of the grated cheese, then season to taste with salt and pepper.

3 Divide the cheesy mixture between the potato shells and place in an ovenproof dish. Sprinkle the remaining cheese over the top and place on a baking tray.

4 Bake in the preheated oven for 20 minutes, or until the cheese has melted and is bubbling, appetizingly crisp and golden brown.

5 Serve sprinkled with chopped spring onions and chives, with some sour cream or yoghurt on the side.

Add some diced ham or crispy bacon.

Good melting cheeses include: mild Cheddar, Swiss cheese (e.g. Gruyère), Fontina, mozzarella, Monterey Jack, Brie and Camembert.

THE COLCANNON SPUD

These traditional Irish creamy mashed potatoes flecked with green cabbage and onions are traditionally eaten on St Patrick's Day. I like to stuff my spuds with a cheesy colcannon filling and enjoy them all year round.

Serves 2 | Prep: 15 minutes | Cook: 30–35 minutes

 **2 x Spud Man baked potatoes**

4 large knobs of butter

85g (3oz) grated cheese

2 tbsp milk or cream (optional)

1 tsp mustard (optional)

a few sprigs of parsley, chopped

chopped spring onions

salt and freshly-ground black pepper

Colcannon filling

1 tsp olive oil

2 tbsp butter

1 small leek, washed, trimmed and thinly sliced

4 spring onions, thinly sliced

1 garlic clove, crushed

¼ small green or Savoy cabbage, cored and thinly sliced (approx. 175g/6oz)

1 Make the colcannon filling: heat the olive oil and butter in a large frying pan set over a medium heat. Add the leek, spring onions and garlic and cook for 5 minutes, stirring occasionally, until tender. Reduce the heat to low and stir in the cabbage. Cook gently, stirring occasionally, for 10–15 minutes, or until softened.

2 Preheat the oven to 200°C (fan 180°C).

3 Cut the cooked spud in half and scoop out the flesh, leaving a 5mm(¼in) thick shell. Transfer to a bowl and mash with 2 knobs of the butter. Stir in the cooked colcannon filling and most of the grated cheese, adding a little milk or cream if needed to slacken the potato. Stir in the mustard (if using) and parsley, and season with salt and pepper.

4 Spoon the mixture back into the potato skins and rough up the tops with a fork. Sprinkle the remaining cheese over the top and place on a baking tray. Bake in the preheated oven for 15 minutes, or until golden brown and bubbling.

5 Serve with butter and chopped spring onions.

THE HUMMUS ONE

Homemade hummus is ridiculously easy to make with tinned chickpeas, and tastes so much better than the stuff you buy in the supermarket. Grilled red peppers add a subtle smoky flavour, while the harissa gives it heat and a vibrant red colour. You can pick up harissa anywhere now.

Serves 2 | Prep: 15 minutes | Sweat: 5–10 minutes

 2 x Spud Man baked potatoes

2 large knobs of butter

a handful of grated carrot

olive oil

paprika (or za'atar or sumac if you want to try something different)

crushed chilli flakes and chopped parsley

salt and freshly-ground black pepper

Red pepper hummus

2 large red peppers

2 x 400g (14oz) tins of chickpeas

3–4 tbsp tahini

4 garlic cloves, crushed

juice of 1 lemon, plus more for drizzling

1–2 tsp harissa paste

1 Make the red pepper hummus: grill the red peppers under an overhead grill, turning them occasionally, until they soften and the skin is blistered and starting to char. Pop them into a plastic bag and leave for 5–10 minutes to sweat. This will make them easier to peel.

2 When the peppers are cool enough to handle, peel them and discard the white ribs and seeds. Cut the flesh into big pieces and place in a food processor or blender.

3 Rinse and drain the chickpeas, reserving the liquid plus a few whole chickpeas for the garnish. Put the rest in the food processor or blender with the peppers.

4 Add the tahini, garlic and lemon juice, and blitz to a coarse purée. Add a little of the reserved liquid and blitz until you end up with a slightly grainy mixture that isn't too smooth, runny or stiff. Stir in the harissa gradually – it's very fiery, so don't add it all at once.

5 Cut a big cross in the top of each spud and press gently on the sides to open it up. Add a knob of butter and season with plenty of salt and pepper. Top with grated carrot and hummus, and drizzle with a little olive oil and some lemon juice. Dust lightly with the paprika and sprinkle with the reserved chickpeas, chilli flakes and parsley.

You can also char the peppers by holding them on a fork over the flame on a gas hob. It's more fun, but you might have to reset the smoke detector more than once.

THE THAI CURRY IN A HURRY

Does what it says on the tin, this. For when you're craving something spicy. I've used frozen prawns, but you can substitute cooked chicken or extra vegetables . . . whatever rocks your boat.

Serves 2 | Prep: 5 minutes | Cook: 20 minutes

 2 x Spud Man baked potatoes

Thai green curry topping

1 tbsp groundnut or olive oil

4 spring onions, thinly sliced

2 garlic cloves, crushed

200g (7oz) mushrooms, quartered

1–2 tbsp green curry paste

200ml (7fl oz) tinned coconut milk

1 tsp Thai fish sauce (nam pla)

grated zest and juice of ½ lime

a large handful of basil or coriander, chopped

200g (7oz) frozen raw king prawns, defrosted

1 red bird's eye chilli, chopped

1 Make the Thai green curry topping: heat the oil in a saucepan set over a low to medium heat. Add the spring onions, garlic and mushrooms and cook, stirring occasionally, for 5 minutes, or until the mushrooms are tender and golden brown.

2 Stir in the green curry paste and cook for 20–30 seconds, then add the coconut milk, fish sauce, lime zest and juice and half of the herbs. Bring to the boil, then reduce the heat and simmer for 8–10 minutes. Add the prawns and cook for 2 minutes until they turn pink.

3 Cut a large cross in the top of each spud and gently squeeze the bottom to open the top. Place each one in a shallow bowl and spoon the curry over the top. Sprinkle with the chilli and remaining herbs and serve immediately.

Use Thai red curry paste instead and add some quartered cherry tomatoes.

THE TUNA DELIGHT

One of the easiest baked spuds ever. Perfect for fans of tuna mayo. I like to flavour mine with lemon juice, but you could stick in horseradish, wasabi, Sriracha or anything that grabs you. Serve these beauties with a crisp salad or some grilled tomatoes.

Serves 2 | Prep: 15 minutes

 **2 x Spud Man baked potatoes**

2 large knobs of butter

60g (2oz) grated cheese

Thai sweet chilli sauce

salt and freshly-ground black pepper

Tuna topping

3 tbsp mayonnaise

juice of ½ small lemon

1 x 145g (5oz) tin of tuna in spring water, drained

150g (5oz) tinned sweetcorn, drained

2 spring onions, chopped

¼ small cucumber, diced

2–3 jarred roasted red peppers, drained and chopped small

a few sprigs of coriander, chopped

1 Make the tuna topping: mix the mayonnaise and lemon juice in a bowl. Break the tuna up into small chunks with a fork and fold gently into the mayonnaise with the sweetcorn, spring onions, cucumber, red peppers and coriander.

2 Cut a big cross in the top of each spud and press gently on the sides to open it up. Scoop out some of the cooked potato inside and mash it with the butter and grated cheese. Season with salt and pepper, and stuff it back into the potato skins.

3 Pile the tuna topping on top of the potatoes and serve, drizzled with sweet chilli sauce.

Instead of using Cheddar, crumble some salty feta over the baked potatoes, and substitute parsley or dill for the coriander.

THE CORONATION CHICKEN ONE

Coronation chicken is usually served as a salad or a sandwich filling, but have you ever tried it as a topping for your baked spuds? It's quick and easy to make and a great way to use up leftover chicken from the Sunday roast. For any Americans out there, it's called 'coronation' chicken because it was created specially for Queen Elizabeth II's coronation in 1953.

Serves 2 | Prep: 10 minutes

 **2 x Spud Man baked potatoes**

2 large knobs of butter

toasted flaked almonds (optional)

salt and freshly-ground black pepper

Coronation chicken topping

5 tbsp mayonnaise

2 tbsp Greek yoghurt

1–2 tsp curry powder or mild curry paste

a pinch of ground turmeric

a pinch of cayenne pepper

2 tbsp mango chutney

2 tbsp sultanas

a handful of coriander, chopped

a good squeeze of lemon juice

225g (8oz) cooked chicken, skinned, boned and cut into pieces

1 Make the coronation chicken topping: put all the ingredients except the chicken in a bowl and mix together well. Check the seasoning, adding more curry powder, ground spices or lemon juice if needed.

2 Gently fold in the chicken. If the mixture is too stiff, loosen it with some more yoghurt.

3 Cut a big cross in the top of each spud and press gently on the sides to open it up. Mash in the butter with a fork and season with salt and pepper.

4 Place each potato in a shallow serving bowl and spoon the coronation chicken mixture into and over the top. Sprinkle with toasted flaked almonds if you have them.

Vary the ingredients: use cooked turkey instead of chicken; substitute dried cranberries or raisins for the sultanas; add some sliced spring onions or chives. This is great served with a crisp green salad.

THE DEVILISH ONE

You can knock up this deliciously sweet and spicy devilled chicken for your baked spuds with some leftover chicken and basic store cupboard ingredients. It doesn't take long to prepare and cook but the longer you marinate it, the fierier it will taste. I'm a devil for big and powerful flavours.

Serves 4 | Prep: 10 minutes | Marinate: 2 hours | Cook: 10–15 minutes

 2 x Spud Man baked potatoes

2 large knobs of butter

1 tsp sesame seeds

thinly sliced red chilli

chopped parsley

salt and freshly-ground black pepper

Devilled chicken

250g (9oz) cooked chicken, skinned, boned and cut into largish pieces

2 tbsp mango chutney

2 tbsp Dijon mustard

1 tbsp Worcestershire sauce

1 tbsp olive oil

2 tsp tomato paste

½ tsp cayenne pepper

½ tsp ground ginger

a good squeeze of lemon juice

a dash of white wine vinegar

1 Make the devilled chicken: cut a few slashes in the pieces of chicken with a sharp knife. Put the remaining ingredients in a bowl and mix well. Add the chicken pieces and turn them gently in the marinade until they are coated all over. Cover and chill in the fridge for at least 2 hours or overnight.

2 Preheat the overhead grill on the highest setting. Arrange the marinated chicken in a foil-lined grill pan or a shallow heatproof dish and grill for 10–15 minutes, turning occasionally, until the chicken is deliciously crisp, sticky and dark brown.

3 Cut a big cross in the top of each spud and press gently on the sides to open it up. Mash in the butter with a fork and season with salt and pepper.

4 Spoon the devilled chicken over the top and sprinkle with sesame seeds. Top with red chilli and parsley, then devour!

 Use cooked turkey instead of chicken — it's a great dish for the Boxing Day leftovers lunch!

SPUDFACTS

Rainbow on a plate:
There are over 4,000 varieties of
potatoes, coming in all shapes, sizes
and even colours like purple and blue.

Incan ingenuity:
The Incas used freezedrying techniques
to preserve potatoes, creating a
product called *chuño*.

Spudland: The largest potato
producer in the world is China,
followed by India and Russia.

THE CURRYWURST SPUD

Currywurst is a popular German street food, and for good reason. Basically, it's sliced pork sausages (any big fat ones will work well) in a sweet and spicy tomato sauce. You're going to love this – it's easy, it's hot, it's spicy, it's meaty . . . what more could you want?

Serves 2 | Prep: 10 minutes | Cook: 15–20 minutes

 2 x Spud Man baked potatoes

2 large knobs of butter

60g (2oz) grated cheese (you could use Gruyère or Emmenthal)

Currywurst topping

4 large pork sausages, e.g. German bratwurst

1 tbsp olive oil

1 small onion, finely chopped

2 garlic cloves, crushed

3 tbsp light brown sugar if using tinned tomatoes (1 tbsp for ketchup)

2 tbsp tomato paste if using tinned tomatoes (1 tbsp for ketchup)

1 x 400g (14oz) tin of chopped tomatoes or 240ml (8fl oz) tomato ketchup

1 tsp red wine vinegar

1 tsp Worcestershire sauce

1–2 tsp curry powder

1–2 tsp cayenne pepper

salt and freshly-ground black pepper

1 Make the currywurst topping: grill or fry the sausages until they are cooked through and browned all over.

2 While they are cooking, heat the oil in a frying pan over a medium heat. Cook the onion and garlic, stirring occasionally, for 6–8 minutes, until softened. Add the brown sugar and stir until dissolved and the onion starts to caramelize.

3 Stir in the remaining ingredients and let the sauce bubble away until it reduces and thickens. If you use tinned tomatoes, you can blend it with a hand blender until puréed and smooth. Season with salt and pepper.

4 Cut a big cross in the top of each spud and press gently on the sides to open it up. Add a big knob of butter and mash it in with a fork, then season with plenty of salt and pepper.

5 Cut the sausages into thick slices and pile on top of the baked spuds. Pour the currywurst sauce over the top and sprinkle generously with grated cheese.

These spuds are so versatile. You can use any vegetables you like, e.g. Mediterranean in the summer and roasted roots in the winter. If you don't have feta, sprinkle with grated cheese or roast some halloumi with the veggies. Increase the spiciness by drizzling with some hot sauce just before serving.

THE VEGGIE DELUXE

These will hit the mark not only for all the vegetarians out there but for anyone who enjoys delicious veg and wants to hit their target of thirty a week. They're good for your innards as well as very tasty and really nice to look at.

Serves 2 | Prep: 15 minutes | Cook: 25 minutes

 2 x Spud Man baked potatoes

2 large knobs of butter

2 large dollops of hummus or tzatziki

½–1 tsp harissa paste (optional)

60g (2oz) feta cheese, crumbled

a handful of crunchy croutons

a few sprigs of basil, mint or parsley, chopped

Seedy roasted vegetables

1 red pepper, deseeded and cut into chunks

1 yellow pepper, deseeded and cut into chunks

1 small red onion, cut into small wedges

300g (10½oz) butternut squash, peeled, deseeded and cubed

4 garlic cloves, in their skins

olive oil

2 tsp mixed cumin and coriander seeds

salt and freshly-ground black pepper

1 Preheat the oven to 200°C (fan 180°C).

2 Make the seedy roasted vegetables: place the prepared vegetables in an ovenproof dish. Tuck the unpeeled garlic cloves in between them and drizzle with plenty of olive oil.

3 Coarsely grind the seeds in a pestle and mortar and sprinkle over the vegetables. Stir gently to coat with the olive oil.

4 Roast in the preheated oven for 25 minutes, or until the vegetables are tender and golden brown but not mushy. Squeeze the roasted garlic out of the skins and mix into the vegetables. Season with salt and pepper.

5 Cut a big cross in the top of each spud and press gently on the sides to open it up. Mash in the butter with a fork and season with salt and pepper. Add a large dollop of tzatziki or hummus to each potato and, if using, swirl in a little harissa – not too much unless you're like me and like super-hot fiery food.

6 Pile the seedy roasted vegetables on top, then sprinkle with the crumbled feta, crunchy croutons and chopped herbs.

THE EGGS FLORENTINE

I go all wobbly for a gooey egg yolk and one of my favourite breakfasts is eggs Florentine. It's incredibly simple but absolutely delicious and will make you as strong as Popeye. I never really go the whole hog and make a classic French hollandaise sauce – it's perfectly decent from a jar.

Serves 2 | Prep: 15 minutes | Cook: 5 minutes

2 x Spud Man baked potatoes

2 big knobs of butter

4 tbsp hollandaise sauce, warmed in the microwave

chopped chives

salt and freshly-ground black pepper

Eggs Florentine topping:

200g (7oz) fresh spinach, washed

1–2 tbsp sour cream or crème fraîche

a pinch of grated nutmeg

4 eggs

1 tbsp white wine vinegar

1 Make the eggs Florentine topping: put the spinach leaves into a colander standing in the sink and pour over two or three kettles of boiling water until it wilts and turns bright green. Press down on it with a small plate or a saucer to squeeze out all the liquid and then transfer to a chopping board and roughly chop.

2 Place the spinach in a bowl with the sour cream or crème fraîche and stir in the nutmeg.

3 Meanwhile, bring a wide pan of water to the boil. Add the vinegar and reduce the heat to a low simmer. Gently crack the eggs, one at a time, into a bowl, then slide them carefully into the simmering water. Poach for 3–4 minutes, until the whites are set but the yolks are still runny. Remove with a slotted spoon and drain on kitchen paper.

4 Cut the cooked spuds in half and scoop out most of the flesh, leaving a 5mm (¼in) thick shell. Transfer the flesh to a bowl and mash it with the butter. Stir in most of the creamy spinach and season with salt and pepper. Spoon the mixture into the potato shells.

5 Place a poached egg on top of each jacket half and pour a spoonful of warm hollandaise over each one. Sprinkle with chives and serve immediately.

You can make a mock hollandaise sauce by whisking 1 tablespoon Greek yoghurt with 3 tablespoons mayo and a dash of wine vinegar or lemon juice.

THE SMOKED SALMON AND CREAM CHEESE ONE

A classic combo this, but the pickled red onion adds a bit of zip. For optimum flavour, use the best smoked salmon you can find. Wild is better and healthier than farmed but it can be expensive. Some supermarkets sell cheaper salmon trimmings, which are perfect for this sort of thing.

Serves 2 | Prep: 15 minutes | Cook: 5 minutes

 **2 x Spud Man baked potatoes**

100g (3½oz) cream cheese

1 tsp horseradish sauce

1 tbsp capers, rinsed and drained

grated zest and juice of 1 lemon

2 knobs of butter

115g (4oz) smoked salmon, thinly sliced

a few sprigs of dill, chopped

salt and freshly-ground black pepper

Pickled red onion

100ml (3½fl oz) red wine vinegar

3 tbsp water

60g (2oz) sugar

a large pinch of salt

1 large red onion, thinly sliced

1 Make the pickled red onion: put all the ingredients except the red onion into a small saucepan set over a low to medium heat and stir well until the sugar dissolves. Turn up the heat and bring to the boil. Let it bubble for 1 minute and then remove from the heat. Stir in the onion and set aside until completely cold. Transfer to a container, cover with a lid and keep in the fridge.

2 Put the cream cheese and horseradish in a bowl and stir gently until well blended. Add the capers and lemon zest and mix well.

3 Cut a big cross in the top of each spud and press gently on the sides to open it up. Add a big knob of butter and season with plenty of salt and pepper.

4 Top with the smoked salmon – you can leave it sliced or cut it into smaller pieces. Trimmings should work as they are. Drizzle with lemon juice and grind some black pepper over the top. Sprinkle with dill and add a large spoonful of the pickled red onion.

The pickled red onions are great for wraps, pitta pockets and even tacos. Make double the quantity and keep in a screw-top jar in the fridge. Substitute some thinly-sliced raw red onion if you don't want to make the pickled ones.

THE CHORIZO SHAKSHUKA

In North Africa, shakshuka is served as a breakfast dish, but it's a good hearty meal any time of day. The chilli and chorizo give it a hot and spicy kick, while the smoked paprika adds warmth. I crumble some salty feta over the top, but you could use Cheddar instead.

Serves 2 | Prep: 15 minutes | Cook: 30–40 minutes

 **2 x Spud Man baked potatoes**

2 big knobs of butter

50g (2oz) feta cheese

salt and freshly-ground black pepper

Shakshuka topping

1 tsp olive oil

½ red onion, diced

1 small red pepper, seeds removed, chopped small

2 garlic cloves, crushed

1 red chilli, seeds removed, chopped small

60g (2oz) chorizo, chopped small

½ tsp smoked paprika

½ tsp ground cumin

1 x 400g (14oz) tin of chopped tomatoes

1 tsp tomato paste

a pinch of sugar

a small handful of coriander, chopped

2 small eggs

1 Heat the oil in a large frying pan over a medium heat. Add the onion, red pepper, garlic and chilli and cook, stirring occasionally, for 5 minutes, or until tender. Add the chorizo and cook for 2–3 minutes. Stir in the ground spices and cook for 1 minute.

2 Add the tomatoes, tomato paste and sugar and simmer for 10–15 minutes, or until the sauce starts to reduce and thicken. Season with salt and pepper and stir in half of the coriander.

3 Preheat the oven to 200°C (fan 180°C).

4 Cut a big cross in the top of each spud and press gently on the sides to open it up as wide as it will go. Add a big knob of butter and mash it in with a fork, then season with plenty of salt and pepper.

If you're not a fan of coriander, use mint, parsley or dill instead.

5 Spoon some shakshuka sauce into each potato and make a hollow in the centre with the back of a spoon. Break an egg into each hollow and place the potatoes on a baking tray. Bake in the preheated oven for 10–15 minutes or until the whites are set and the yolks are still slightly runny.

6 Transfer the potatoes to shallow serving bowls and pour the remaining shakshuka sauce over them. Crumble the feta over the top and sprinkle with the remaining coriander.

POSH BAKED BEANS

Fancy a taste of the Mediterranean on top of your spuds? Here's another delicious Greek-style dish that is basically posh baked beans – cheap, healthy and easy to make. And if you leave out that all that lovely butter, they're vegan! The Greeks use large dried white beans called *gigantes* but dried butter beans work well, too.

Serves 2 | Prep: 15 minutes | Soak: overnight | Cook: 1¼ –1½ hours

 2 x Spud Man baked potatoes

2 knobs of butter (optional)

a handful of parsley or mint, chopped

115g (4oz) feta cheese, crumbled

Posh baked beans

300g (10½oz) dried *gigantes* or butter beans

4 tbsp olive oil

1 onion, finely chopped

2 celery sticks, finely chopped

2 garlic cloves, crushed

2 tbsp tomato paste

675g (1½lb) juicy ripe tomatoes, skinned and coarsely chopped

leaves from a few oregano sprigs (or dried)

1 tsp sugar

1 tbsp red wine vinegar

salt and freshly-ground black pepper

1 Put the beans in a large bowl, cover with cold water and leave to soak overnight.

2 The following day, drain the beans, then rinse under running cold water and transfer to a large saucepan. Cover with plenty of cold water and bring to the boil. Reduce the heat to a simmer and cook gently for 45–50 minutes, until the beans are slightly tender but still retain some bite. Do not overcook them – they must not be soft or mushy. Drain in a colander, reserving the cooking liquid.

3 Preheat the oven to 170°C (fan 150°C).

Did you hear about the evil baked potato?
His plans were foiled.

4 Heat the olive oil in a saucepan set over a medium heat. Cook the onion, celery and garlic, stirring occasionally, for 6–8 minutes, or until tender. Stir in the tomato paste and cook for 1 minute. Add the drained beans, tomatoes, oregano, sugar, vinegar and 400ml (14fl oz) of the reserved cooking liquid. Stir well and season with salt and pepper.

5 Transfer to a large ovenproof baking dish or roasting pan and cover with kitchen foil. Bake in the preheated oven for 1 hour, then remove the foil and cook for 20–30 minutes, or until the tomato sauce has thickened and the beans are tender. Leave to cool at room temperature – they are best eaten lukewarm.

6 Cut a big cross in the top of each spud and press gently on the sides to open it up. Add a knob of butter (if using) and season with plenty of salt and pepper. Spoon the beans over the top and sprinkle with chopped herbs and crumbled feta cheese.

If you have any leftover beans, serve them on toast or at room temperature with some cold meats, chicken or cheese.

EASY CHEESY POTATO SKINS

Guaranteed cheese-pull on this one. Oozing with melted cheese and topped with crispy bacon — what's not to love? Eat these skins as a snack or pass them round at parties. Don't throw away the scooped-out potato — mash it with some milk and butter and reheat it for tomorrow's supper.

Serves 3–4 | Prep: 10 minutes | Cook: 10 minutes

2 x Spud Man baked potatoes

100g (3½oz) streaky bacon or pancetta, chopped

100g (3½oz) grated cheese

8 heaped tsp sour cream or Greek yoghurt

2 spring onions, thinly sliced

a few chopped chives

salt and freshly-ground black pepper

These skins taste delicious served with some spicy tomato salsa or drizzled with chilli sauce or pesto. Or dust with cayenne or chilli powder.

1 Preheat the oven to 200°C (fan 180°C).

2 Cut the cooked spuds in half and spoon out some of the flesh to leave a hollow in the centre. There should be about 5mm (¼in) potato left inside each skin to form a shell. Season lightly with salt and pepper.

3 Set a non-stick frying pan over a medium to high heat and cook the bacon or pancetta, turning occasionally, for 3 minutes, or until crispy and golden brown.

4 Fill the shells with the cooked bacon and grated Cheddar and place on a baking tray. Cook in the preheated oven for 6–8 minutes, or until the shells are golden brown and the cheese has melted and is bubbling.

5 Top each potato skin with a dollop of sour cream or yoghurt and sprinkle with spring onions and chives. Serve immediately.

SPUD MAN

PLAIN
WITH BUTTER

CHEESE

BBQ PULLED PORK

SWEETCORN

TUNA MAYO

COLESLAW #homemade

BEANS

CHILLI CON CARNE #homemade

#homemade

CHICKEN CURRY

MINCED BEEF

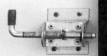

PIZZA LOADED POTATO SKINS

It doesn't get much better than this. The only thing that can make a spicy pizza better is spuds. Customise it with your favourite foods: anchovies, a jar of roasted red peppers, fried mushrooms or black olives. You name it.

Serves 3–4 | Prep: 5 minutes | Cook: 8 minutes

 *2 x Spud Man baked potatoes*

8 tbsp tomato or pizza sauce (tinned, bottled or homemade)

200g (7oz) shredded mozzarella

85g (3oz) diced or sliced pepperoni

a few basil leaves, torn

salt and freshly-ground black pepper

1 Preheat the oven to 200°C (fan 180°C).

2 Cut the cooked spuds in half and spoon out some of the flesh to leave a hollow in the centre. There should be about 5mm (¼ inch) potato left inside each skin to form a shell. Season lightly with salt and pepper

3 Put a spoonful of tomato sauce into each shell and scatter the shredded mozzarella over the top. Sprinkle with the pepperoni and place on a baking tray.

4 Bake in the preheated oven for 8 minutes, or until they are golden brown and the cheese has melted and is bubbling.

5 Serve immediately, sprinkled with the basil leaves.

Don't throw away the scooped-out potato – mash it with some milk and butter and reheat it for tomorrow's supper.

LOADED BAKED POTATO NACHOS

If you like traditional Tex-Mex nachos made with tortillas, you're going to love my version made with good old baked spuds. This is also a great way to use up any leftover cold spuds from the day before. As if there will be any!

Serves 6 | Prep: 15 minutes | Cook: 15 minutes

4 x Spud Man baked potatoes, cold

2 tbsp olive oil

1 tbsp butter

1 tbsp taco seasoning

200g (7oz) grated cheese

6 spring onions, chopped

¼ red onion, chopped small

3 juicy ripe tomatoes, chopped small

1 avocado, peeled, stone removed, chopped small

a handful of coriander, chopped

salt and freshly-ground black pepper

To serve (optional)

spicy tomato salsa

guacamole

sour cream

a few drops of Sriracha or Tabasco

lime wedges

1 Preheat the oven to 220°C (fan 200°C).

2 Cut the spuds into rounds, about 5mm ((¼in)) thick.

3 Heat the oil and butter in a large frying pan set over a high heat. Add the potatoes in a single layer (you may need to do this in batches) and cook for 2–3 minutes on each side until golden brown and crispy round the edges. Remove from the pan and drain on kitchen paper. Season lightly with salt and pepper.

4 Spread the potatoes out on a large baking tray with a rim. Dust with the taco seasoning and sprinkle the grated cheese over the top.

5 Bake in the preheated oven for 10 minutes, or until the potato edges are crispy and the cheese has melted.

6 Top with the onions, tomato, avocado and coriander, adding some salsa, guacamole or sour cream, if wished. To make the nachos really spicy, drizzle with Sriracha or Tabasco.

These nachos are very versatile and
you can add your favourite toppings
and flavourings, e.g. black beans or kidney
beans, refried beans, minced beef or vegan
chilli, bottled jalapeños, chopped fresh chillies,
red or green peppers, tinned sweetcorn
or black olives.

Serve warm with lime
wedges for squeezing Everyone
can just help themselves and
dig in!

TUNA MELT SPUDS

My take on tuna melt toasties. Swap the bread for spuds and you'll never look back. This will soon be a firm family favourite and you can knock it up for your tea with a little (all right, a lot of) cheese and some store cupboard staples.

Serves 2 | Prep: 10 minutes | Cook: 15 minutes

 2 x Spud Man baked potatoes

Tuna melt topping

15g (½oz) butter

60g (2oz) grated cheese

3 spring onions, thinly sliced

1 x 145g (5oz) tin of tuna in spring water, drained and flaked

a few sprigs of parsley, chopped

4 tbsp tinned sweetcorn, drained

salt and freshly-ground black pepper

1 Preheat the oven to 200°C (fan 180°C).

2 Cut the cooked spuds in half and scoop out the flesh, leaving a 5mm (¼in) thick shell. Transfer the flesh to a bowl and mash with the butter. Season with salt and pepper and beat in most of the cheese, reserving a spoonful for the top, then stir in the tuna, parsley and sweetcorn.

3 Spoon the mixture into the potato shells and place on a baking tray. Sprinkle with the reserved grated Cheddar.

4 Bake in the preheated oven for 15 minutes until the shells are golden brown and the cheese has melted.

5 Serve piping hot.

Serve this with a crisp green salad: Cos or Little Gem lettuce, cucumber, avocado and chopped parsley.

RED ONION AND GOAT'S CHEESE SKINS

These posh spud skins are oozing with goat's cheese and sweet, sticky caramelized onions. Great for snacks, drinks, barbecues and parties. Don't throw away the scooped-out potato — mash it with butter, milk, garlic, chopped herbs and grated cheese or use as a topping for a pie. Nothing goes to waste in Spud Man's home.

Serves 3–4 | Prep: 15 minutes | Cook: 45–55 minutes

4 x Spud Man baked potatoes

8 thin slices of soft goat's cheese, e.g. chèvre or goat's cheese log

crumbled crispy bacon

chopped chives

salt and freshly-ground black pepper

Caramelized red onions

15g (½oz) butter

2 tbsp olive oil

2 large red onions, thinly sliced

3 garlic cloves, crushed

1 tbsp red wine vinegar

2 tbsp light brown sugar

1 Make the caramelized red onions: heat the butter and olive oil in a large frying pan set over a low heat. Add the onions and cook very slowly and gently for 30–40 minutes, stirring occasionally, until they are tender and golden brown and starting to caramelize. Watch them carefully in case they start to burn.

2 Stir in the garlic and cook for 1 minute, and then add the vinegar and sugar. Cook gently for 5 minutes, stirring until the sugar dissolves.

3 Preheat the oven to 200°C (fan 180°C).

4 Cut the cooked spuds in half and spoon out some of the flesh to leave a hollow in the centre. There should be about 5mm (¼in) potato left inside each skin to form a shell. Season lightly with salt and pepper.

5 Divide the caramelized red onions between the potato shells and place a slice of goat's cheese on top of each one. Arrange them on a baking tray.

6 Bake in the preheated oven for 6–8 minutes, or until the goat's cheese is golden brown and starting to bubble.

7 Serve hot, sprinkled with crumbled crispy bacon and chives.

SPICY GUAC AND SHRIMP SKINS

These spicy loaded skins are a real treat. You can make the guacamole in advance (or use a tub of fresh guac from the supermarket) and then throw everything together when the potatoes are cooked. As always, keep the scooped-out potato and use it up later, perhaps with some bangers, fried onions and gravy.

Serves 3–4 | Prep: 20 minutes | Cook: 5 minutes

4 x Spud Man baked potatoes

30g (1oz) butter

450g (1lb) large prawns, peeled (see tip)

2–3 tsp Cajun seasoning

3 garlic cloves, crushed

a few sprigs of parsley, chopped

sliced jalapeños or crushed chilli flakes

salt and freshly-ground black pepper

Guacamole topping

1 red chilli, chopped small

½ red onion, chopped small

2 garlic cloves, crushed

½ tsp sea salt crystals

2 ripe avocados, peeled and stones removed

juice of 1 lime

1 small bunch of coriander, chopped

1 ripe tomato, seeds removed, chopped small

freshly-ground black pepper

Do not overcook the prawns or they will go hard. You can use frozen and defrosted raw tiger or king prawns, which are ready to eat as soon as they turn from grey to pink on both sides. Or you can use cooked prawns and just reheat for 2–3 minutes each side until golden.

Lighten up:
A medium baked potato only has about 100 calories.

1 Make the guacamole topping: crush the chilli, onion, garlic and salt in a pestle and mortar or using the back of a large knife.

2 In a bowl, mash the avocados roughly with a fork and stir in the lime juice, coriander and crushed chilli and onion mixture. Add the tomato and mix everything together. Season with black pepper and set aside.

3 Melt the butter in a large frying pan over a medium to high heat. Add the prawns and Cajun seasoning and stir well until the prawns are coated all over. Add the garlic and cook for 4–5 minutes, or until the prawns are cooked right through. Stir in the chopped parsley and remove from the pan.

4 Cut the cooked spuds in half and spoon out some of the flesh to leave a hollow in the centre. There should be about 5mm (¼in) potato left inside each skin to form a shell. Season lightly with salt and pepper.

5 Fill the potato shells with the guacamole and Cajun prawns. Sprinkle with some sliced jalapeños or chilli flakes and serve.

SAUSAGE AND MASH LOADED SKINS

A new take on a classic. I just can't get enough of them and neither will your family and friends. And there's no need to miss out if you're a veggie — you can make them with Quorn sausages instead.

Serves 3–4 | Prep: 15 minutes | Cook: 15–20 minutes

4 x Spud Man baked potatoes

plenty of mustard, e.g. English, Dijon, honey mustard

hot sauce or ketchup (optional)

salt and freshly-ground black pepper

Sausage filling

8 chipolatas (plain or flavoured with leeks, herbs, etc.)

30g (1oz) butter

2–3 tbsp milk

115g (4oz) grated cheese

1 Cook the sausages in an oiled frying pan over a medium heat or under a preheated overhead grill, turning them occasionally, for 6–10 minutes, until cooked right through and browned all over. Slice them into chunks.

2 Preheat the oven to 200°C (fan 180°C).

3 Cut the cooked spuds in half and spoon out some of the flesh to leave a hollow in the centre. There should be about 5mm (¼in) potato left inside each skin to form a shell. Season lightly with salt and pepper.

4 Put the scooped-out potato in a bowl and mash with the butter and milk. Season with salt and and stir in two-thirds of the grated cheese. Lastly, gently stir in the sausages.

5 Spoon the mixture into the potato shells and place on a baking tray. Sprinkle the remaining cheese over the top.

6 Cook in the preheated oven for 8–10 minutes until the shells are golden brown and the cheese has melted and is bubbling.

7 Serve with plenty of mustard and, if wished, drizzle with hot sauce or ketchup.

You could stir the mustard into the
sausage and mashed potato mixture
before loading and cooking the skins.

CREAMY CHEESY TWICE-BAKED BRIE POTATOES

I eat these gorgeous buttery spuds oozing with melted cheese all year round, but they are particularly good for using up any leftover Brie and cranberry sauce over the Christmas holiday. They even look festive with their red, white and green colours. Any creamy cheese will work – try Camembert or Gorgonzola too.

Serves 2 | Prep: 10 minutes | Cook: 15 minutes

 **2 x Spud Man baked potatoes**

2 large knobs of butter

chopped spring onions or chives

sweet paprika or cayenne

caramelized red onion chutney or cranberry sauce

Creamy cheesy Brie filling

100g (3½oz) ripe Brie, rind removed and chopped small

100g (3½oz) sour cream

2 garlic cloves, crushed

3 spring onions, finely chopped

a few chives, finely chopped

salt and freshly-ground black pepper

Try adding some chilli flakes or drizzle with Sriracha or sweet chilli sauce. If you're feeling posh (and flush) drizzle with some truffle oil.

1 Preheat the oven to 190°C (fan 170°C).

2 Make the creamy cheesy Brie filling: put most of the Brie in a bowl and add the sour cream, garlic, spring onions and chives. Season with salt and pepper.

3 Cut the cooked spuds in half and scoop out the flesh, leaving a 5mm (¼in) thick shell. Transfer to a bowl and mash it with the butter. Stir in the creamy cheesy Brie filling and check the seasoning.

4 Spoon the mixture back into the potato skins and dot with the remaining Brie. Place on a baking tray and bake in the preheated oven for 15 minutes, or until the cheesy topping is golden brown and bubbling.

5 Serve sprinkled with spring onions or chives and dusted with paprika or cayenne with some caramelized red onion chutney or cranberry sauce. Fantastic!

THE AVERAGE ANNUAL POTATO CONSUMPTION PER PERSON WORLDWIDE IS 3.5KG. IT SHOULD BE MORE.

TEX-MEX LOADED SKINS

These cheesy bean skins are loaded with veggies and really colourful. You'll definitely get your five-a-day! I like to top them with a fiery hot salsa and some smashed up avocado. Don't forget to save the scooped out mashed potato — it'll keep in a covered container in the fridge for 24 hours.

Serves 3–4 | Prep: 15 minutes | Cook: 8–10 minutes

4 x Spud Man baked potatoes

1 ripe avocado, peeled and stone removed

1 garlic clove, crushed

juice of ½ lime

a few drops of olive oil

a pinch of crushed chilli flakes

spicy tomato salsa

Cheesy bean filling

100g (3½oz) fresh spinach, washed

150g (5½oz) tinned black beans, rinsed and drained

4 spring onions, thinly sliced

1 hot red chilli, chopped small

115g (4oz) grated cheese (you could try Monterey Jack)

salt and freshly-ground black pepper

1 Make the cheesy bean filliing: put the spinach leaves in a colander standing in the sink and pour over one or two kettles of boiling water until they wilt and turn bright green. Press down on the spinachwith a small plate or a saucer to get rid of all the liquid and then transfer to a chopping board and roughly chop.

2 Transfer to a bowl and mix with the beans, spring onions, chilli and most of the grated cheese. Stir well and season to taste with salt and pepper.

3 Preheat the oven to 200°C (fan 180°C).

What's a potato's favourite TV show?
Starch Trek.

4 Cut the cooked spuds in half and spoon out some of the flesh to leave a hollow in the centre. There should be about 5mm (¼in) potato left inside each skin to form a shell. Season lightly with salt and pepper.

5 Spoon the cheesy bean filling into the potato shells and sprinkle the remaining cheese over the top. Place them on a baking tray and bake in the preheated oven for 8–10 minutes, or until the cheese melts and is golden brown and bubbling.

6 Meanwhile, put the avocado, garlic, lime juice, oil and chilli in a bowl with some salt and pepper and roughly mash with a fork until well combined but still slightly lumpy.

7 Serve the potato skins topped with the smashed avocado and salsa.

You could use kidney beans or tinned refried beans instead of black ones. Serve with a bowl of Greek yoghurt or sour cream.

THE ONE, THE ONLY, ALL-DAY BREAKFAST SPUD

If you're like me and love a Full English, you can enjoy these blowout breakfast spuds at any time of the day. They look and taste amazing – a real showstopper! Just what you need after a hard night.

Serves 2 | Prep: 10 minutes | Cook: 15 minutes

 2 x Spud Man baked potatoes

2 big knobs of butter

4 tbsp grated cheese

chopped parsley or chives

mustard, ketchup, brown sauce or Worcestershire sauce

salt and freshly-ground black pepper

Breakfast topping

2 large pork sausages

2 small tomatoes, halved

1 tsp olive oil

4 bacon rashers

150g (5½oz) mushrooms, thickly sliced

2 hash browns

2 eggs

1 tbsp white wine vinegar

1 Preheat the overhead grill and place the sausages on a foil-lined grill pan. Pop under the hot grill and cook, turning occasionally, for 8–10 minutes, or until they are cooked through and appetizingly brown all over. Remove and keep warm in a low oven.

2 Halfway through cooking the sausages, pop the tomatoes under the grill and cook for 4–5 minutes, or until softened and starting to brown. Remove and keep warm.

3 Meanwhile, heat the oil in a large frying pan over a medium to high heat and fry the bacon rashers for 1–2 minutes each side until golden brown and crisp. Remove and keep warm with the sausages and tomatoes.

4 Add the mushrooms to the pan and cook, stirring occasionally, for 4–5 minutes until cooked and golden. If needed, add some more oil or a little butter. Remove and keep warm.

5 Cook the hash browns according to the instructions on the packet.

SHOWSTOPPER!

6 Meanwhile, bring a pan of water to the boil. Add the vinegar and reduce the heat to a low simmer. Gently crack the eggs, one at a time, into a bowl, then slide them carefully into the simmering water. Poach for 3–4 minutes, until the whites are set but the yolks are still runny. Remove with a slotted spoon and drain on kitchen paper.

If you have an air fryer, preferably with a double drawer, it's easy to cook the sausages and bacon in one drawer, and the mushrooms and tomatoes in the other.

As always, make your own tweaks to this recipe. Fry the eggs instead of poaching them; or try adding black pudding, baked beans or even some crisp fried breadcrumbs. Anything goes.

7 Cut a big cross in the top of each spud and press gently on the sides to open it up. Add a big knob of butter and mash it in with a fork, then season with plenty of salt and pepper.

8 Place each potato on a serving plate and top with the mushrooms and bacon. Slice the sausages and cut the tomatoes and hash browns into quarters, then add to the topping. Don't worry if some of the topping tumbles over the side on to the plate! Scatter with the grated cheese and top with a poached egg. Finish with a sprinkle of parsley or chives and get stuck in! Pierce the egg with your fork and let all the lovely runny yolk run out over the topping and on to your plate. Serve with mustard, ketchup, Worcestershire sauce or brown sauce.

SPUD

Spudding nora: Believe it or not, the potato isn't a root, but an underground stem called a tuber.

Ancient eats: People in the Andes have been enjoying potatoes for over 7,000 years.

Spudding it away: The average American consumes about 140lb of potatoes per year. That's nearly 65kg.

Spuds in space: In 1995, the potato became the first vegetable ever grown in space.

Royal spuds: French Queen Marie Antoinette was known to wear potato blossoms in her hair. Let them eat spuds!

Potassium powerhouse: A single potato boasts more potassium than a banana.

Spudurable: When stored properly in a cool, dark place, potatoes can last up to a year.

Spud name: The potato's scientific name is Solanum tuberosum, meaning 'nightshade' and 'swollen.'

Don't gotta be green: Those green spots on a potato? They contain a toxin called solanine and shouldn't be eaten.

Bug repellent power: Studies have shown that potato peelings can be used as a natural bug repellent.

Not spuds: Though both are called potatoes, sweet potatoes are actually a completely different vegetable.

Spud museums: Believe it or not, there are several museums dedicated to potatoes, notably the Idaho Potato Museum.

Electric taters: Potatoes can be used to power a light bulb. They contain enough phosphoric acid to generate electricity.

Global grub: The potato is the fourth most important food crop in the world by total production.

FACTS

A potato is about 80% water and 20% solids.

The US Department of Agriculture has stated that 'a diet of whole milk and potatoes would supply almost all of the food elements necessary for the maintenance of the human body.'

More than 1 billion people worldwide eat potato, and more than 375 million metric tons are grown worldwide.

China grows 25% of the world's potatoes.

There are over 180 wild potato species.

Around 80 varieties are sold commercially in the UK.

Potatoes can grow from sea level up to 4,700m above sea level.

One hectare of potato can yield two to four times the food quantity of grain crops.

Potatoes are 78% water. Until I add butter.

It takes 14 days on average for a potato seed to sprout.

Potatoes produce more food per unit of water than any other major crop and are up to seven times more water-efficient than cereals.

Potatoes do NOT count as one of your five fruit and veg a day according to the National Health Service.

Mr Potato Head, the toy, was invented in 1949. It was the first toy advertised on television.

SPUDJOKES

★ ★ ★ ★ ★

What do you call a lazy spud?
A couch potato!

What do you call a reluctant potato?
A hesitater.

What do you get when it rains potatoes?
Spuddles.

What do you call a spinning potato?
A rotate-o.

How does a potato win at video games?
It mashes the buttons.

Why was the potato so quiet?
It was a medi-tater.

Why do potatoes make good detectives?
Because they always keep their eyes peeled.

What do you call a fake potato?
An imi-tater.

What do you call a potato with right angles?
A square root.

What do you call a potato at a football game?
A spec-tater.

Why was the potato in court?
It wanted to a-peel.

What instrument does a spud play?
A tuber.

Why did the potato cross the road?
Because there was a fork up ahead.

What do you call a baby potato?
Small fry.

Why was the spud wearing socks?
To keep his pota-toes warm.

What type of potato starts arguments?
An agi-tater.

What did the father potato say to his daughter before her football game?
I'm rooting for you.

ACKNOWLEDGEMENTS

To Sarah and the kids: I love you more than taters.

To Grandad Bernard, thanks for many hours of adventures on the farm growing up. Your advice is still invaluable to me today.

To Grandma Joan, still the best maker of pancakes in the world — I miss you each day and know you would be so proud of me.

To my Dad, Michael, potato merchant to many! Dad who would have loved every second of all that has happened. Always there to help, even when you yourself were not well. I miss you.

And to the renal team at the Royal Derby, and particularly the home dialysis team, without whom I couldn't do any of what I do. Here's to you Berrnan Rivera, Carol Rhodes, Chris Swan, Geoff Inacay and Dr Richard Fluck.

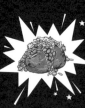